Gallery Books
Editor: Peter Fallon

THE LOVES OF CASS McGUIRE

THE
LOVES
OF
CASS
McGUIRE
BRIAN FRIEL

Gallery Books

This edition of
The Loves of Cass McGuire
is first published
in paperback and in a
clothbound edition
by The Gallery Press
in December 1984.

The Gallery Press
19 Oakdown Road
Dublin 14, Ireland.

ISBN 0 904011 60 7 (*paper*)
0 904011 61 5 (*clothbound*)

All performing rights in this play are strictly reserved. Applications should be addressed to Curtis Brown, 162-168 Regent Street, London WIR 5TA. The Gallery Press receives financial support from The Arts Council / An Chomhairle Ealaíon, Ireland, and acknowledges the assistance of The Arts Council of Northern Ireland in the publication of this book.

Author's Note

In my description of the set I mention that the winged chair is never used throughout the play except during the three rhapsodies. These occur, one in each Act, as part of the formal pattern or ritual of the action; and the musical term, rhapsody, seemed to me to be the most accurate description of them. Each of the three characters who rhapsodize — Trilbe, Ingram and Cass — takes the shabby and unpromising threads of his or her past life and weaves it into a hymn of joy, a gay and rapturous and exaggerated celebration of a beauty that might have been. (And to pursue the musical imagery a stage further, and as a signpost for future productions, I consider this play to be a concerto in which Cass McGuire is the soloist.)

When I wrote the play I envisaged these rhapsodies being played against a musical background; and I chose Wagner because his *Tristan Und Isolde* legend has parallels of sorts in Cass McGuire's story. But during rehearsals I discovered that two of the actors spoke their rhapsodies with such grace and dignity, invested their soliloquies with such cantabile magic, that any background music would have been a distraction. So Wagner was dropped. But I have left the directions for the music in the text because subsequent companies may not be so fortunate in their rhapsodists and they may be grateful for the potent crutch that the *Liebestod*, for example, affords.

Brian Friel

The first performance of *The Loves of Cass McGuire* was presented at the Helen Hayes Theater, New York, on 6 October 1966 by the David Merrick Arts Foundation. It was directed by Hilton Edwards, and the setting was by Lloyd Burlingame. The cast was as follows:

MOTHER	Frances Brandt
DOM	Don Scardino
ALICE	Sylvia O'Brien
HARRY	Liam Redmond
CASS	Ruth Gordon
TESSA	Mary Greaney
PAT QUINN	Arthur O'Sullivan
TRILBE COSTELLO	Brenda Forbes
MR INGRAM	Dennis King
MRS BUTCHER	Dorothy Blackburn

The first European performance of the play was given at The Abbey Theatre, Dublin on 10 April 1967. It was directed and set by Tomás Mac Anna; and the cast was as follows:

HARRY McGUIRE	Patrick Layde
ALICE	Máire Ní Néill
DOM	Desmond Cave
CASS	Siobhán McKenna
MOTHER	May Craig
TRILBE COSTELLO	Joan O'Hara
MR INGRAM	Bill Foley
PAT QUINN	Mícheál Ó h-Aonghusa
MRS BUTCHER	Peggy Hayes
TESSA	Máire Ní Ghráinne

Time: the present in Ireland.

Act I   Two weeks before Christmas. Morning.
Act II   One week before Christmas. Afternoon.
Act III   Christmas Eve. Evening.

Cast

HARRY McGUIRE
DOM McGUIRE   Harry McGuire's youngest son
MOTHER   His mother
ALICE   His wife
CASS   His sister
TESSA   Maid in Eden House
PAT QUINN
TRILBE COSTELLO
MR INGRAM
MRS BUTCHER   All residents in Eden House

Set

A spacious, high-ceilinged room, somewhere between elegance and
austerity, which serves as the common-room in Eden House, a
home for old people, and also as the living-room in the home of
Harry McGuire, a wealthy Irish businessman-accountant.

The back wall consists of glass and French windows which open
out to a formal garden where a Cupid statue (illuminated) is frozen
in an absurd and impossible contortion.

A large marble fireplace on wall right (from the point of view of
the audience). Round mahogany table centrestage. Two fireside
chairs and several upright chairs.

Downstage right, conspicuous in its isolation, is a big, winged
armchair. This is never used throughout the play except during the
three rhapsodies.

Upstage left, on a raised platform, is a bed, bedside-table, and a
chair. This area will be Cass's bedroom in Eden house. It will be
black when the curtain first rises.

for Nano and Mary

Act One

When the curtain rises, GRAN McGUIRE, *Harry's mother, is sitting in her wheel-chair, and young* DOM *is huddled over the fire, reading a True Detective comic.* GRAN *is eighty-nine and almost totally deaf. Black satin blouse, a rug around her knees, and a black shawl which has fallen from her shoulders. Were she able to walk around she would have the authority and self-possession of a queen; but because she is invalided she just looks monumental. The serene, superior expression on her face never varies because nothing can touch her now. Her speech is slow and dignified.*

DOM, *aged seventeen, wears flannels and a school blazer. He is too big physically to be a schoolboy and not yet a young man, and is conscious of his gaucheness.*

He looks furtively at the door, takes a cigarette from his pocket, lights it, and inhales ostentatiously. Then goes on reading.

MOTHER The next question is an easy one. Hands up any child who can tell me the name of the new cardinal. Anyone in the class know?

DOM Captain Mike O'Shea, Vice-Squad Headquarters, 47th Precinct.

MOTHER I beg your pardon?

DOM 'O'Shea flung his men around the building and dashed inside. The startled Samoan girls in varying forms of undress ran screaming into Madam Lulana's.' Wow-wow-wow-wow!

MOTHER I'm afraid you'll have to raise your voice a little.

DOM You're a deaf and doting old bag of guts. D'you know why Madam Lulana kept only Samoan girls? Because all they think of is sex, Gran — just like you and me. And no matter what climate they're in, they never wear under-clothes.

MOTHER And I'm told that Cardinal Logue is a brilliant classical scholar, too.

DOM   I'll tell you a secret, Gran: when I leave school, I'm going to set up a business of my own, right here in town — a kip house. And I'll make you the madam. And anyone that tries to get too smart, you'll give them the old knee in the groin — one-two-three — Gorgeous Gran McGuire, The Sailors' Terror!

MOTHER   I want everyone to repeat that ten times.

DOM   Gorgeous Gran McGuire, The Sailors' Terror; Gorgeous Gran McGuire, The Sailors' Terror; Gorgeous Gran McGuire, The Sailors' . . . .

He breaks off when he hears his mother approach left. Throws the cigarette into the fire, after a desperate effort to nick it, and dashes back to the table where his school books are impressively arrayed. Sticks the True Detective into his jacket pocket. He is studying when his mother enters.

ALICE *is in her fifties. She is expensively, but not attractively, dressed. She notices* DOM'S *scramble to get a school book opened. She is carrying chairbacks for the fireside chairs.*

ALICE   I thought you were studying.

DOM   Gran and I were discussing the hierarchy.

ALICE   I hear your father's car. Put your books away and take your grandmother with you into the dining-room.

DOM   Lunch ready?

ALICE   Yours is. We aren't eating until later.

DOM   What about Auntie Cass?

ALICE   Still asleep.

DOM   Can I bring up her tray?

ALICE   No.

DOM   I've bought a bar of chocolate for her.

ALICE   I said she's asleep.

DOM   No wonder. I could hear her singing at the top of her voice half the night.

ALICE   That'll do, Dom.

DOM   She must be feeling terrible today. Just as well Madam Gran is deaf. (*Articulating into* GRAN'S *ear*) She called you, her own mother, A Big Cow!

ALICE Dom, please!
MOTHER You'll not forget this day.
DOM (*Solemnly*) It's engraved on our hearts in letters of gold.

> *Enter* HARRY *left. Good black coat, soft hat, carrying a paper. He is sixty but looks younger. A measured middle-of-the-road man, well in control of himself. He has his mother's soft attractive voice. He gives* ALICE *a perfunctory kiss, hands her the coat and hat, and sits at the fire.*

ALICE You're late, aren't you?
HARRY I had a few calls to make. How are you today, Mother? Dom?
ALICE Will you have a drink?
HARRY Brandy, please. And nothing in it.
ALICE You and I are having a light lunch.
HARRY ?
ALICE The Traynors are coming to dinner tonight.
HARRY Hell.
ALICE (*Leaving*) They're your friends.
HARRY (*To* DOM) How's the work going?
DOM All right.
HARRY I phoned the college and told them you had a cold. (*Pause*) How is it?
DOM All right.
HARRY You're sure you don't want a grind during the Christmas holidays?
DOM No . . . no. . . .
HARRY I can get young Coyle to come to the house, you know.
DOM No, it's . . . all right.
HARRY A matter for yourself. (*Nods and smiles at* GRAN) Mother.
MOTHER They tell me the beaches are crowded.
HARRY It's freezing outside.
MOTHER I'm thinking seriously of investing in a parasol.

> ALICE *enters with a drink and a letter. She hands both to* HARRY.

13

ALICE A letter from Betty. They bought that house after all.

HARRY How much?

ALICE Seventeen thousand.

HARRY Very nice.

ALICE And they're coming for Christmas . . . with the baby.

HARRY That's good news. We'll have a full house. (*Opening letter*) Mother seems to think it's summer.

ALICE She has been teaching me Latin roots all morning. Anything fresh downtown?

HARRY Not a thing. Here?

ALICE All quiet so far.

HARRY She hasn't appeared yet?

ALICE Not a sound. Did you find out where she was? What happened?

HARRY Where was she not. I called in Sweeney's pub on the way home and paid for the breakages. Apparently every table in the lounge was an antique.

ALICE And the police?

HARRY The sergeant was with me. I squared that. Dom!

ALICE And the clay on her shoes — how did she get it?

HARRY Bring my brief-case in from the car, son, please.

ALICE You've got to do something, Harry.

The subdued domestic atmosphere is suddenly and violently shattered by CASS'S *shouts. She charges on stage (either from the wings or from the auditorium) shouting in her raucous Irish-American voice. Everyone on stage freezes.*

CASS *is a tall, bulky woman of seventy. She wears a gaudy jacket (because of the cold weather) over gaudy clothes; rings; earrings; two voluminous handbags which never leave her. She smokes incessantly and talks loudly and coarsely (deliberately at times). Ugly is too strong a word to describe her, and plain not nearly strong enough. If she ever had good features once, there is no trace of them now. A life of hard physical work has ravaged her. Only her spirit is strong and resilient.*

CASS What the hell goes on here?

ALICE Cass — !

HARRY Cass, you can't break in, Cass, at — !

> CASS *addresses the audience directly. They are her friends, her intimates. The other people on stage are interlopers.*

CASS Cass! Cass! Cass! I go to the ur-eye-nal for five minutes and they try to pull a quick one on me!

HARRY The story has begun, Cass.

CASS The story begins where I say it begins, and I say it begins with me stuck in the gawddam workhouse! So you can all get the hell outa here!

HARRY The story begins in the living-room of my home, a week after your return to Ireland. This is my living-room and we're going to show bit by bit how you came —

CASS (*Looking around set*) Sure! Real nice and cosy! (*Directly to audience*) The home of my brother, Mister Harold McGuire, accountant, brick manufacturer, big-deal Irish businessman. Married to Alice, only child of Joe Connor, the lawyer, who couldn't keep his hands off young girls.

HARRY That's enough, Cass!

CASS Four kids: one a lady doctor; one an architect; one a clergyman; and one a student — if I may say so. What else do they (*audience*) need to know?

ALICE Harry, for heaven's sake — !

CASS (*Looking around*) Yeah, this'll do for the workhouse. We have swank windows, too, opening out on to a garden, only we don't have a nekked kid holding his hands in front of his rice crispies all day.

HARRY This isn't fair to us, Cass. It must be shown slowly and in sequence why you went to Eden House.

CASS I didn't go, Harry boy, I was stuck in! Oh, sure, sure, go back and show them how patient you all were with the terrible woman that appeared out of the blue after fifty-two years! — how her momma doesn't reconnize her, and how her brother is embarrassed by her, and how Alice — Jeeze, yes — I think poor Alice is afraid of her! You afraid of me, Alice?

15

ALICE Harry — !

HARRY Cass, I insist we unfold the story in proper sequence!

CASS And then this day she goes and visits her father's grave
— that's how she got the clay on her shoes, sweetie —
and then gets plastered and kicks up a bit of a shindy in
a downtown bar, and someone calls the cops, and
someone keeps screaming, 'It's Mr. McGuire's sister,
the returned Yankee!' and then her folks have this big
solemn meeting — I just saved you all that — and decide
to stick her into the workhouse and —

HARRY Eden House is a rest home for elderly people.

CASS Listen to him! He could sell fur coats to chow dawgs in
the Sahara. So we're going to skip all that early stuff, all
the explanations, all the excuses, and we'll start off later
in the story — from here. (*Light up bed area*) My suite in
the workhouse, folks. Drop in and see me some time,
okay? Where the hell was I? (*Remembering*) Yeah — the
homecoming — back to the little green isle. Well, that's
all over and done with — history; and in my book yesterday's dead and gone and forgotten. So let's pick it up
from there, with me in the . . . rest home. (*To* HARRY *who
is about to go off stage*) Go ahead and call out the
National Guard if you like; but you're not going to move
me! What's this goddam play called? *The Loves of Cass
McGuire.* Who's Cass McGuire? Me! Me! And they'll
see what happens in the order *I* want them to see it; and
there will be no going back into the past!

MOTHER The present Chief Justice is a past pupil of mine.

CASS And I'm Garibaldi's mistress. And this ain't no visiting
day in Eden House. So get the hell outa here, all of you.
Go on, go on; clear. You, too, professor (DOM). The less
you see of your old Auntie Cass the better, because she
ain't got no money, and we suspect she doesn't go to
church, and we're not too sure if she's a maiden aunt at
all. (ALICE *quickly signals to her family to leave*)

HARRY You'll regret this, Cass.

CASS I regret nuthin'.

HARRY You may think you can seal off your mind like this, but
you can't. The past will keep coming back to you.

CASS I live in the present, Harry boy! Right here and now!

HARRY We have a point of view, too, and in fairness to all of us — (*At the word 'fairness' she makes an extravagant dismissing gesture with her hand*)

CASS Aaaaaaaaagh!

She moves into her bedroom and sits on the bed. HARRY *holds a brief consultation with his family, and apparently they decide to go away because they move off. Now that she is alone with the audience, her friends,* CASS *is more subdued. She talks to them almost confidentially. But the past scene has disturbed her more than she would like to admit: her hands are shaking. She fumbles for a cigarette and lights it. Then she makes up. During all this business she addresses the audience.*

CASS Well, that stirred things up a bit, dinnit? The past . . . poof! (*To herself in the hand mirror*) Ugh! It's not like whiskey, beautiful; the years don't improve it. (*Remembering*) Like there was this bum used to come in for breakfast every morning into this joint on the Lower East Side I worked in. Boy, you should ov seen his hands! Joe Bolowski, that was his name; they said he was a concert pianist or something before he messed hisself up. Anyways, Joe would look at me like I was the blazing July sun or something, and he would say, 'Honey, I pulled the chain on better-looking things'. Asked me to marry him, too. Every Friday night. When he was drunk. (*Producing half-bottle of whiskey from one of the bags*) Hellova guy, Joe. (*Drinks straight from bottle*) To the future. . . . Shhhh.

INGRAM *appears outside French windows. After a few seconds he is joined by* COSTELLO.

CASS See that? That's old Ingram. She's probably there with him — Trilbe Costello. Trilbe — now there's a name for you! I sez to her the first day, 'You some kind of hat or something?' They're gooks, okay, real gooks, phew. . . . He played the organ in some swank English cathedral, he tells me; and she was — you know — a professor of speech and elocution and all that crap. Real swank. Always talking about poetry and music and stuff. And as Pat Quinn sez — you'll see him around, too; a good guy, Pat — as he sez, you'd think they'd be past all that now, wouldn't you? Kinda sweet though, aren't they? And there's something about old Ingram, I dunno, maybe it's the quiet way he talks but he reminds me of Harry.

In the gloom immediately beyond Cass's bed HARRY *appears in his dressing-gown and slippers. He talks softly, gently, and* CASS *answers him in a remote tone at first. He looks at her but she stares straight down into the auditorium. This is the first of the memory sequences that haunt Cass. Some of them she keeps at bay by talking resolutely to the audience. But some are so potent that she is seduced into re-living them.*

HARRY You should have let me run you out in the car, Cass.
CASS I wanted to be alone.
HARRY The grave's nice. And the flowers. Alice planted them.
CASS Pretty flowers.
HARRY We got a stonemason up from Cork to do the headstone.
CASS I sent ten dollars. All I had at the time.
HARRY Apparently Father had been living for over twenty years in a . . . sort of doss-house, right in the centre of Glasgow. They lived in a two-roomed flat on the ground floor.
CASS Three weeks buried before I even knew.
HARRY He must have told this woman he was a widower because she asked me how long Mother was dead. I didn't . . . tell Alice that.
CASS (*Briskly to audience*) There was this guy owned the joint I worked in. . . .
HARRY He looked much older than seventy-six. The woman said he had been invalided for the last five years.
CASS — I told you about it — a breakfast counter. . . .
HARRY Oh, yes, I forgot: she said Father talked a lot about his daughter, Cass.
CASS Jeff Olsen was his name. And he had this dawg, see, this

18

bitch, and we lived in this two-roomed apartment. . . .

HARRY What age were you when he went away, Cass? Fifteen? Sixteen?

CASS — and when that bitch would get high she would yap-yap-yap, and all the dawgs in the block they would yap-yap-yap back — O Jeeze — until everyone was screaming murder.

HARRY I was only five when he left. I have no memory of him at all.

CASS So, Jeff, first he got that bitch de-sexed; and then when that done no good he got it de-barked — you know, so that it couldn't bark no more; and there was this bum, Slinger, from down South, sometimes he took coffee in our joint, and when Jeff told him about the dawg being de-sexed and de-barked, Slinger said, 'Nothin' left for it but to dee-cease, Jeff'. Real funny guy, you know. . . .

HARRY She knew all about his job on the old railway, and how you would hide in the signal box with him when you should have been at school with Mother.

CASS (*Brutally*) That's finished! All over!

HARRY *drifts into the darkness of the wings.*

CASS And I don't go in for the fond memory racket! For fifty-two years I work one block away from Skid Row — deadbeats, drags, washouts, living in the past! Washing, scrubbing, fixing sandwiches — work so that you don't have no time to think, and if you did you thought of the future. (*Fumbling greedily for the bottle*) The past's gone. Good luck to it. And Gawd bless it. (*Drinks. Then lights another cigarette*)

TESSA, *the maid, enters from the right. She is distributing clean pillow-slips for the beds. The boredom and drudgery of working with old people have made her weary at eighteen. She is untidy (until Act Three) and protects herself from the senility around her by an acquired casualness of manner. When she sees her* CASS *hides the bottle.*

19

TESSA You're almost a week in the house now and you know fine well you're not allowed in your bedroom between breakfast and teatime.

CASS Sweet little Tessa.

TESSA And another thing: unless you're sick, you're supposed to be down in the oratory for Mass in the morning.

CASS What time's that at?

TESSA Seven.

CASS I'm always in the DTS till ten at least.

TESSA Will you move? How can I fix the bed with you on it?

CASS You've got a point there.

While TESSA *changes the pillow-slip* CASS *gathers her things to go to the common-room.*

TESSA Are you a bed-wetter?

CASS Only when I'm waiting to be raped, sweetie.

TESSA *goes off left.* CASS *goes upstage. At the same time* PAT QUINN *enters right. A small, plump man. Assured, confident, cunning. The know-all of the institution. Anxious to please. In his early sixties.*

CASS Hi, Pat.

PAT How are you, Miss McGuire?

CASS Where is everybody?

PAT All in bed, pretending they're sick, on account of the cold weather.

CASS Ain't they got no peat around here now?

PAT The boiler's busted. But by the time they get round to fixing it, I'll be gone — back to the nephew's farm.

CASS (*Not listening, searching bag*) You bet.

PAT He has 500 acres and 350 head of cattle. I'm only temporary here, you know, until himself and the missus move into the new house.

CASS Same here. I'm temporary, too.

PAT He's chairman of the Young Farmers' League.

CASS Big deal.

PAT And I keep an eye on the men when he's away at the meetings.

CASS You going downtown today, Pat?

PAT I'm on my way out now for the papers.

CASS You know that store right next the post-office?

PAT What place is that now?

CASS The first store below the post-office on the same side.

PAT Is it Sweeney's pub you're talking about?

CASS You go in there and ask the bartender — Tommy's his name — you ask him for the same again for Miss McGuire.

PAT The same again . . .?

CASS And have one on me outa the change.

PAT Is it . . . drink . . . for you?

CASS It's not baby powder I'm looking for!

PAT Holy God, if the matron caught me at that game!

CASS (*Taking back money*) Gimme. Someone else'll get it for me.

PAT No, no, it's all right. A wee drop now and again is good for the health.

CASS That's it, Pat. Look at the woman it made of me.

TRILBE COSTELLO *bursts in, followed by* MR. INGRAM. *She is in her early seventies but is full of energy. She has been an elocution teacher all her life — but without the necessary qualifications and consequently never recognized by the education department — and her speech and manner both reflect this: she articulates fanatically and is inclined to domineer. At the same time one is conscious of an insecurity behind the extravagant exterior.* MR. INGRAM *is a small, withered, testy, nervous old man. He is English. He is so frail and hesitant that he seldom finishes a sentence. He carries large volumes with him everywhere he goes. Now, as they enter,* TRILBE *is consulting some sheets of paper and at the same time addressing an imaginary group of people.* CASS *is still new to* TRILBE *and views her with open wonder.* PAT *knows* TRILBE *well and humours her.*

TRILBE Before I announce the results of the competition I would like to take this opportunity to thank all those young boys and girls who came up here so bravely and spoke their test piece with such courage and gusto. A very sincere thank you to you, indeed.

PAT There you are, now.

CASS Hi.

TRILBE (*Softly*) Morning. Morning. I'm adjudicating at a speech festival for junior schools next week. Just a little rehearsal.

CASS Sure, sure — you just blast ahead.

TRILBE You know *The Highwayman*, don't you?

CASS Which one? Where I worked they were all —

TRILBE 'The wind was a torrent of darkness among the gusty trees

The moon was a ghostly galleon tossed upon cloudy seas . . .'

PAT There's speaking for you!

TRILBE Noyes.

CASS Well, maybe just a little —

TRILBE Alfred J. Noyes. Not his best but it fires the young imagination. Next Thursday. You're welcome if you choose to come. (*Adjudicating again and moving slowly off*) I liked in particular competitors number 7, 8 and 13 whose sense of rhythm stirred me. 'Tlot-tlot in the empty silence, tlot-tlot in the echoing night'. Thrilling.

INGRAM It is our experience . . . we find . . . we find that one doesn't feel the cold so . . . so . . . if one keeps on the move and doesn't. . . .

TRILBE Mr. Ingram!

INGRAM Coming, Miss Costello. We walk round past the refectory and along the . . . it's a very pleasant little . . . good morning. . . .

CASS *looks after them as they exit right.*

CASS Boy, would Ed Sullivan eat them up!

PAT Adjudicating! That one — sure she wasn't even qualified to teach that elocution stuff! Running about the countryside from the nuns to the brothers, scrounging meals and picking up an odd shilling here and there. A tramp with notions — that's what that one is!

CASS (*Mopping her face*) Can she spit!

PAT The Costellos from Ardbeg — didn't I know them all in my day. All high-falutin' chat and not a penny to scratch themselves with. Your mother there could tell you all about them.

CASS I'm sure *she* could. You going downtown, Pat, or are you not?

PAT (*Leaving*) I'll be back in ten minutes. The same again for Miss McGuire. And no one'll know a word about it. By the way, boiled bacon for dinner, and stewed apples after.

He exits. CASS *sits down in the common-room, lights a cigarette, and addresses the audience.*

CASS Wonderful! And prunes for breakfast. All I need now is to go on a rum bash. Funny title, too, innit? *The Loves of Cass McGuire* — like I was Mata Hari or something. I'm seventy, by the way. And Harry, he's pushing sixty. And momma, she's . . . gee, momma must be eighty-nine now . . . yeah . . . 'cos Father he was three years older than her. He sailed off when I was a kid — just to fill you in on the background — 'cos momma and him didn't hit it off too well when he took a drop. Never wrote nor nothing. Just got hisself lost in Scotland. So, when I was eighteen, I kinda got the same idea, you know; not that momma and me didn't hit it off; we got on okay, I guess, but. . . . Well, what the hell was there to do around here, I mean. Oh boy, she raised Cain, I'll tell you; real schoolteacher stuff; sent for Father O'Neill to speak to me and all. . . . (*Remembering*) Now, whatever happened to him? Dead, I guess. He was some guy, you know: big and heavy and this voice like a fog-horn. Should ov been in the marines. (*Laughs gently*) The night he caught Connie Crowley guzzling the hell outa me below the crooked bridge! 'You bastard,' he sez — well, mebbe he didn't use that word — 'Are you comfortable in your sinning?' And poor Connie, Jeeze I could feel his knees going, he sez, 'Please, no, Father. The grass's damp.' Anyways, I saved up and gathered the passage money

23

and left a note for momma and one for Connie . . . and
off I blew . . .(*looks around the room*) and back I come
home to my own people — and they have this big solemn
meeting — and decide to kick me out!

HARRY *strides on from right, his coat across his arm.
He is very stern but tries to control himself. She is
aware of what he is saying to her but talks on resolutely
to the audience.*

HARRY I've just been told what happened this morning, Cass.
CASS So now you know it all.
HARRY And I will not have you insult Alice about her father.
CASS Harry's four kids, boy, they got on good: Betty, she's a
doc in London, and Tom's a priest, and Aidan's an
architect, and Dom —
HARRY But this is only the last of many, many insults.
CASS Fine kids — I haven't met them yet — but you'll see,
they'll be along one of these days to meet their Auntie
Cass —
HARRY And before I say any more I want you to know that the
decision I've made is entirely my own. Alice had nothing
to do with it.
CASS Betty, she has a baby — fourteen months — I seen
pictures of it.
HARRY In fact she has just asked me not to mention this until
after Christmas.
CASS (*Unable to hold her own line*) So I left a note for momma
and one for Connie. . . .
HARRY But I said no, definitely no.
CASS They tell me Connie's a big-shot in Dublin now — two
department stores and married and all and a chauffeur-
driven car. . . .
HARRY And I can tell you that Dom is missing none of your
antics, and at his impressionable age, too.
CASS So I left a note for him, see; one for him and one for
momma; but he must never have gotten his.
HARRY But that's all finished, all finished. And to get back to my
decision —

CASS *cannot fight the memory any longer. She suddenly wheels wildly round to him. She almost screams her lines.*

CASS Say out what you're trying to say, Harry! Speak up and say it out straight!
HARRY Cass, I've come to the decision —
CASS Well?

ALICE *appears at the door left,* DOM *and* MOTHER *at the door right.* CASS'S *volume drops rapidly.*

HARRY I've arranged for you to go into Eden House next Monday.
CASS Where?
HARRY It's a rest home for elderly people, at the end of the town, near the black church.
ALICE Harry, I asked you to wait until —
CASS That the workhouse?
HARRY It's where the workhouse used to be.
ALICE There's no urgency, Cass. You can stay with us — over Christmas.
CASS (*Incredulous*) Jeeze, the work—
HARRY It's not the workhouse. It's a rest home.
CASS (*Totally broken*) I'm not going.
HARRY Every week the bank will pay your board and send you an allowance.
CASS I'm not going.
ALICE They're very particular about who they take in there, Cass.
HARRY And you're under no obligation whatever to me. You're entirely independent.
CASS I haven't a dime.
HARRY Your own money will support you adequately.
CASS I haven't a dime.
HARRY It's all intact.
CASS I'm not going.
ALICE Any time you feel like coming out to visit us . . . .
CASS (*In desperation*) Momma. . .?
MOTHER You'll remember this day.

25

CASS Dommie boy. . . ?
DOM I'll call on my way from school every —
HARRY Dom! You're too sensible to make a scene, Cass.

She surveys them slowly. Pause.

CASS Next Monday?
ALICE I think we should wait until after —
HARRY Next Monday. It's all settled.

CASS turns her back on them and talks to the audience. She is still very, very subdued. The brashness has vanished.

CASS (*Searching for any words*) Monday for wealth, Tuesday for health, Wednesday the best day of all; Thursday for crosses, Friday for losses. (*Driving herself into a sort of gaiety*) I wear sneakers, you know, with the toes cut out 'cos my feet, boy, they sure give me hell standing behind that counter. Fine on a Monday morning, and not too bad on Tuesday, but by Wednesday — Jeeze — way up like this; and for the rest of the week they're throbbing like they had the neuralgia. (*The others drift out quietly*) And this doc I go to, boy, is he a comedian, he sez: You gotta spend the mosta the day in a recumbent posture. No filthy cracks, Mister, I sez; in case you haven't noticed I'm a lady, 'cos I thought he was making his move. But Jeff he told me what the doc meant, and when I knew what it was, I just laughed — you know — serving coffee in a recumbent posture! . . . Hell, this is no fun for you, huh? No way to make friends and influence people. *The Loves of Cass McGuire* — huh! Where did he get that title from anyways? (*Rising to her feet. As if confused*) Where have all the real people gone?
INGRAM (*Off: reading*) 'At that time young Tristan lived at the court of his uncle, King Mark.'

Immediately she hears TRILBE *and* INGRAM *approaching,* CASS *pulls open her bag, takes out a compact, and powders herself rapidly.*

26

CASS Abbott and Costello again! Maybe they'll give us a laugh.

They enter. INGRAM *is reading from one of the books he always carries and* TRILBE *is listening to him attentively.*

TRILBE We've been round three times. I feel positively intoxi-cated.

CASS Boy, you're lucky.

INGRAM 'And there he captivated everybody with his good looks and his minstrelsy. . . .'

CASS Don't he get tired doing the mobile library act?

TRILBE (*Confidentially*) His Wagner, m'dear. Won't trust them with anyone.

CASS Wagner?

INGRAM You know Wagner?

CASS Do I know Wagner! Voted for him every election.

INGRAM Elect— ?

CASS Best mayor New York ever had.

TRILBE There you are. It's a small world, isn't it. By the way, m'dear, what *is* your Christian name?

CASS Cass.

TRILBE Cass? Cass? It's certainly not Cass. (*To* INGRAM) Did you ever hear of anyone being christened Cass?

CASS I was baptized Catherine.

TRILBE Agh, Catherine! Now we have it! I'll call you Catherine and I insist you call me Trilbe. (*Softly*) His Christian name is Meurice. He is convinced his father did it to him on purpose.

CASS Couldn't we call him Buster or something?

TRILBE (*Seriously assessing the name*) Buster. . . .

CASS Or what about . . . yeah, Pop! Huh?

TRILBE I don't think he'd like that, m'dear. He has been Mr. Ingram for so long now. (*Aloud*) Continue reading, Mr. Ingram. (*Softly*) His explosives are very vital —

CASS Gee. . . .

TRILBE — but his vowels are inclined to be flabby.

CASS Oh, I'm sorry to hear —

INGRAM (*Irritably*) If you would only keep quiet.

TRILBE Nobody's saying a word. (*Softly*) I've my adjudication

27

almost ready.

CASS Yeah?

TRILBE It should be quite impressive. Shhhhhh.

INGRAM 'But in a duel with the warrior Morhol he was seriously wounded and went to Ireland to recuperate.'

TRILBE I can't hear you. Catherine can't hear you. More chest. More lungs.

INGRAM 'And there he met Isolde, the daughter of the Queen —'

TRILBE Better.

INGRAM '— who ministered to him and tended him and restored him to former vigour.'

CASS (*To audience*) Jeeze, didn't I tell you!

INGRAM 'But when his uncle, King Mark, was told of the beauty of Isolde, he dispatched Tristan to fetch Isolde for himself, and Tristan reluctantly set out to do the king's bidding. As he was bringing her back by boat both he and Isolde drank by mistake the potion which was to make them inseparable lovers.'

CASS (*To audience*) What the hell's keeping Pat Quinn with my potion of hooch!

TRILBE (*Cosily*) It's the part about the exile I like best.

INGRAM 'The king married Isolde, and although his spies were constantly on the look-out, she and Tristan met frequently in secret. But finally the king learned of their trysts and exiled Tristan to the coast of Brittany.'

TRILBE Ah!

INGRAM. 'And there he married another Isolde but his love was always for the first, the Irish, Isolde. Eventually, having been wounded again. . . .'

CASS (*To audience*) That guy should ov bought hisself accident insurance.

At this TRILBE *gets to her feet and comes over to* CASS. *She has got to play the following sequence on two levels at once: she is her normal, vital self, inquisitive and anxious to help; and at the same time she must convey the first inklings of an 'otherness', of the private world she and* INGRAM *have created and take refuge in occasionally.*

28

TRILBE M'dear, who *are* you addressing?

CASS You just carry on. I'm sorta — you know — having an odd word with the folks out there. (*Indicates audience*)

TRILBE Who?

CASS The folks.

> TRILBE *shades her eyes against the footlights and searches the auditorium. She looks back at* CASS *and again at the auditorium. She sees no one out there.*

TRILBE Catherine, m'dear, we are your only world now. We have the truth for you.

CASS Yeah?

TRILBE Join with us, Catherine, for we have the truth.

CASS Sure . . . sure. . . .

INGRAM May I?

TRILBE We know what is real, Catherine.

INGRAM Does anybody wish to listen?

TRILBE Mr. Ingram, I'm going to sit in the winged chair.

INGRAM It's almost lunch-time and —

TRILBE I haven't sat in it for three whole weeks, and now I wish to remember.

INGRAM I really think you ought to wait until —

TRILBE The past, and all the riches I have, and all that nourishes me.

INGRAM Very well, Miss Costello.

TRILBE Mr. Ingram knows my story. And I know his. And we tell our stories to one another occasionally when we're alone. . . .

> *She sits in the winged chair. Very gently bring up Wagner's* Venusberg *music (omit first two minutes of it).* TRILBE *and* INGRAM *relax into the mood and respond to one another.* CASS *is not in their sphere. She watches and listens alertly, cautiously, nervously.*

I was called Trilbe because I was born the year the book was published; and Father loved it so much — he was so romantic — and he was so fond of Paris. And it was spring time, and he and I were travelling in Provence —

INGRAM In the south of France.

TRILBE — and we were spending a few days in Arles when I met him, Gordon —

INGRAM Gordon McClelland.

TRILBE — from Edinburgh. And Father was so proper, you know; so proper and so stern, poor Father.

INGRAM And what is your profession, young man?

TRILBE I love your daughter, sir; I love your daughter, Trilbe.

INGRAM I see. I see.

TRILBE Father always said that when he was puzzled. And in the afternoons, when he would go to his room to rest, Gordon and I would walk hand in hand along the country roads —

INGRAM Between the poplars.

TRILBE — in the shafts of golden sun; and every so often we would stop, and he would touch my face with his fingertips and whisper to me —

INGRAM My little golden Trilbe.

TRILBE And I would tremble with delight at his gentleness and his beauty and his love for me. And when we married we bought a château —

INGRAM On the banks of the Loire.

TRILBE — and had servants and music and wine and still days of sun and children with golden hair, named after princes and princesses; and we travelled and travelled and travelled — Russia, India, Persia, Palestine — never stopping, always moving —

INGRAM My little golden Trilbe.

TRILBE — sleeping in strange beds, eating strange food. . . .

INGRAM Good-bye . . . good-bye. . . .

TRILBE Travelling, moving, visiting strange places, meeting new people, with Gordon beside me.

INGRAM My little golden Trilbe.

TRILBE And the servants and the music and the wine and the travel and the poetry and his love for me and my love for him . . . all so real. My Gordon from Arles on the Loire, my prince from Edinburgh in Provence . . . my father resting in the afternoon, my journeys to the Nile and the Volga, the road to Samarkand, the road, the traveller's road. . . .

30

INGRAM Trilbe.

TRILBE Gordon McClelland.

INGRAM Golden Trilbe.

TRILBE My highland prince.

INGRAM My little golden Trilbe.

TRILBE Say it slowly after me: 'But I, being poor, have only my dreams. . . .'

INGRAM Our truth.

TRILBE — 'I have spread my dreams under your feet.
Tread softly because you tread on my dreams.'

INGRAM Our truth.

TRILBE Love was his profession. And Father was such a sensible man. (*She rises slowly to her feet and offers her arm to* INGRAM) You may lead me to the dining-room, Mr. Ingram.

INGRAM My pleasure.

> *He takes her arm and they exit like a king and his queen. The music fades with them.* CASS *stares in naked astonishment after them. She is still gaping at the exit left when* DOM *appears in the shadows right. She does not turn to face him but answers him automatically: she is still thinking of what has happened.*

DOM Psst! Auntie Cass!

CASS Hi. . . .

DOM Did you live with Jeff Olsen, the man that owned the place you worked in, Auntie Cass?

CASS (*Nodding yes*) Poor good Jeff . . . lost a leg in the Great War. . . .

DOM Were you ever married to him?

CASS Had a wife somewhere on the west coast. . . .

DOM Did you sleep with him?

CASS And when the pain in the missing leg got real bad I stroked his forehead. . . .(*At this* DOM *laughs coarsely and darts into the wings.* CASS *turns round front. Calling softly, vaguely*) Jeff? . . . Jeff? . . . Connie?

> *Enter* PAT *left.*

PAT I could smell the bacon on the street. Boys, but I could eat a horse.

CASS Hi, Pat. . . .

PAT Are you all right? There's nothing wrong with you, is there?

CASS Pat, tell me, Pat, what did her father do?

PAT Whose father?

CASS Trilbe Costello's.

PAT He was a French polisher by trade but he couldn't hold a job. Never sober. Ended up as a sort of caretaker out at the greyhound track. Always wore wellingtons and a greasy bowler hat. Your mother could tell you all about —

CASS Did she travel?

PAT Didn't I tell you! Never lit — running from one school to the next, and hoping for a square meal.

CASS Or married — was she ever married to a guy from Scotland?

PAT For God's sake, woman, she wouldn't know the difference between a bull and a clucking hen! What the hell's come over you?

CASS I dunno, Pat. Jeeze, I dunno.

PAT You're foundered with the cold. Here's the stuff'll put some life into you. (*Produces bottle*)

CASS Yeah . . . yeah . . . phew!

PAT Have you a glass in your bag?

CASS I don't need a glass. Boy, is this a gook joint! Jeeze, a girl would want to have her wits about her here! (*To audience*) Gordon! What d'you know! Almost had me fooled, too. (*To* PAT) But I can handle gooks — spent a lifetime handling gooks. Skid row, I'll tell you, it was full of them, full of them. . . .(*She drinks from the bottle*) . . . And I'll handle this, too, Pat, huh?

PAT *is watching her cautiously. He decides it is best to humour her, just as he did earlier with* TRILBE.

PAT Here's your change.

CASS Keep it. You bet, they'll not wear Cass McGuire down, huh?

32

PAT You're looking better already.

CASS No siree. I'll ride this gook joint.

PAT Now you're talking.

CASS By Jeeze, I'll ride it, Pat, huh.

PAT That's fighting language!

CASS And I'll beat it, too, Pat.

PAT I'm with you there.

CASS We'll beat it together, Pat!

PAT Up the Republic!

CASS Together, Pat, we'll beat it, boy! It'll not get us down. No siree!

Quick Curtain. End of Act One.

Act Two

When the curtain rises, CASS *is sitting on her bed, making up Christ-mas parcels. A miniature Christmas tree sits on the pillow. She is smoking and has a bottle at hand. She talks directly to the audience.*

CASS Hi. I made damn sure to be in possession this time. I'll tell you. And I hope you don't get the 'flu from me 'cos nearly everybody in this joint got it — even matron; and, boy, the bug that put her on her back deserves a citation. Buster Ingram, he got it too, and Pat, and most of the folks in the upper wing. Me — I took precautions. (*Drinks*) But the whole house is kinda depressed, you know. That's why I fixed this (*tree*) up for the common-room and bought a couple of presents. Not that I ever went in for this Christmas schmalz. Hell, we open Christ-mas morning at 5.30 same as usual; probably the busiest morning in the whole year; and the stream of poor bastards coming howling for black coffee — you should ov seen them! Happy Christmas — Jeeze! (*Softly*) But one Christmas night, 19 and 42 it was, Jeff and me were

33

sitting listening to the radio or something, and Jeff he jumps up and sez, 'Hell, Cass, I almost forgot!', and he hobbles into the kitchen and comes back with this tiny box, and he sez, 'Here', like it was burning him; and I opens it, and there's this brooch, made like it was a shamrock with three leaves and all, and with green and white and orange diamonds plastered all over it — only they were glass, I guess. And, hell, I dunno what happened to me; maybe I was drunk or something; but I began to cry. And poor Jeff he didn't know where to look, and he shouted, 'Jeeze, Cass, I gave some Irish bum a ham and cheese sandwich for it day before yesterday. You don't think I *bought* it?' And, Gawd, I cried all the more then . . . must ov been real drunk . . . you know, he was so kind to me. . . . (*Raucously*) Hell, I hate Sundays!

Enter TESSA *with a brush and dust-pan.* CASS *hides the bottle.*

TESSA Look at the mess the floor's in!
CASS I'll clean it up.
TESSA Some people were reared in a byre. (*Picks up one of the presents, a spray of artificial flowers*) Aw, isn't that lovely!
CASS Like it?
TESSA They're nicer than real.
CASS Yeah.
TESSA And I have a pink dress, too.
CASS Well. . . .
TESSA Would you ever?
CASS What?
TESSA Give them to me.
CASS (*Gently*) Sweetie, I wouldn't give you the time of day.
TESSA You dirty, mean aul' pagan! (*So refined*) Thanks be to God *I* was at Mass this morning.

She swaggers off and CASS *watches her with amusement.*

CASS There goes a walking saint. It's (*the flowers*) for Trilbe;

and these gloves are for Buster Ingram; and I got socks (*holds one up*) for Pat. I thought they went in pairs, these things. (*She finds the other*) They do. Poor guy, always talking about that nephew of his taking him away. Some nephew, I'll tell you. Which reminds me of something he was telling me the other day: Ingram's married! What d'you know about that! (*Looks around before she continues*) He was only a young guy, see, slashing away at the organ in his swank English cathedral, and this day in comes this hoofer from a nearby music-hall — you know — a dancer, flinging her legs up and making guys sweat. Anyways, Buster he sees her and falls hard for her and can't let her outa his sight, not even for a second. . . . (*Checking mentally: this has not occurred to her before*) But I ask you, what the hell was the hoofer doing in the swank cathedral in the first place? Mebbe her feet was hurting her. Anyways, old hot-rod Ingram he throws up the organ-bashing and follows the variety troupe she's in all over England! And his father — he was a judge or something — he goes chasing after Buster; and his momma she goes chasing after his father. Must ov been like the Keystone Cops. But finally in some hick town on the coast he gets her to marry him. And two days after the wedding what does she do? Sails off with some German count that has a yacht there! Never seen her again. How about that! (*Tailing off vaguely*) I guess it was the title tickled her . . . and the yacht . . . Count and Countess . . . Countess Connie . . . The Bastard! Anyways, she sailed away, and forgot everything and never came back again, and maybe that's what I should ov done. But I came back to Ireland and got such a welcome that, Jeeze, I thought for ten minutes I was Santa Claus!

> HARRY *enters. He is wearing slippers and is dressed in a cardigan. He has just had his evening meal and is relaxed. He sits beside the fire.* CASS *continues to address the audience.*

HARRY Lord, it really is wonderful, Cass, to have you back. I —

I just can't believe it!

CASS She was a hoofer, but what the hell was her name. . .?

HARRY The trouble is I've so much to tell you and so much to ask you that I don't know where to begin.

CASS Anyways, she sailed away for ever. . . .

HARRY Fifty-one years — my God, it's a lifetime.

CASS Fifty-two.

HARRY And yet I distinctly remember the morning you went away. I ran up to the back attic — remember the back attic with the window you pushed open with the iron bar?

CASS Six slots in it. . . .

HARRY And I threw myself across your bed and cried my heart out.

CASS Harry . . . I don't want to remember.

HARRY D'you know, I was convinced my heart was literally crushed!

CASS Please . . . please, Harry, let me forget.

HARRY We were always so close to one another, Cass. Always. I thought the sun rose and set on you. Welcome home a thousand times.

Now, for the first time, CASS wheels round and almost runs into the common-room. She is ecstatic with joy. She wanders about the common-room, looking at it, looking at HARRY, laughing foolishly.

CASS Home! I can't even begin to tell you what this means to me, Harry. This is what it was all for — to come home again. You and Alice and the kids — Jeeze, Harry, I hope it's not too much for me — you know — like a high-ball on an empty stomach.

HARRY We'll make up for all the lost years, Cass.

CASS And what a home. I'm so glad for you, Harry, I can't tell you. (*Enter ALICE with a tray of drinks*) And Alice! You know you're just like you are in all those pictures. Hell, you were only — what! — a pollywog in a cot when I left, but I knew your father okay.

ALICE Everybody knew Father.

CASS Joe Connor? For Gawds sakes every evening we'd be

36

coming home from school we'd meet him at the courthouse steps and he'd call one of us over and . . . (*suddenly realizing*) and . . . he'd say, 'How are youse, girls?' . . . Oh, a real gentleman, Mr. Connor, with his gold chain across here and his butterfly collar —

ALICE You must be exhausted after the flight. Would you try a little sherry?

CASS I'll try anything — whiskey for preference. Tell me, how's the kids?

ALICE Great.

CASS When am I going to see them?

ALICE We don't see a lot of them ourselves, but they'll all come flocking now.

CASS Father Tom still teaching away at the high school?

ALICE Didn't you know? He's left the seculars. In the Jays now.

CASS Yeah?

ALICE For the past three and a half years.

CASS Gawd! Can't the docs do nothing for him?

HARRY The Jays — the Jesuits, Cass.

CASS Jeeze, I thought she said the jakes!

HARRY I'm going to propose a toast.

CASS Lovely!

HARRY To Cass and to the future.

CASS I'll drink to that.

HARRY And I want to say this, too: this is your home now, Cass; look on yourself as one of the family.

ALICE Come and go as you wish.

CASS And I want to propose a toast. (*Recalling*) Hold on now — Sliocht sleacht ar shliocht do shleachta.

ALICE German?

CASS Hell, it's supposed to be gawddam Gaelic, and it means . . . I forget — May your offspring have offspring — or something.

HARRY Why did you never marry out there?

CASS Me?

ALICE We often thought you might have married the proprietor of the restaurant you were manageress in.

CASS The rest — ? Oh, Jeff Olsen! Hell, Jeff and me were too pally to get married, you know. A sweet guy, but as I used to say to him: 'Jeff, boy, I want a man with his two feet on the ground'.

HARRY He was a successful businessman, wasn't he?

CASS Sure. But he had only one leg. Who's for more swill? (*She pours herself another drink*)

ALICE Did you mention the party to her?

HARRY I didn't have a chance yet.

CASS What's that?

HARRY We were talking of having a welcome-home party for you.

CASS Wonderful! I can still dance. (*She lifts her skirt and does a few steps of an old-time waltz as she hums her own accompaniment*) And I'll sing, by Gawd, if the neighbours don't object! (*Sings*)
'Oft in the stilly night ere slumber's chains have bound me
Sad memory brings the light. . . .'
Aw, hell, I haven't sang since the night James Michael Curley was buried!

ALICE You're a caution, Cass.

CASS This party — who's coming?

HARRY We'll have the Traynors and the Kirks and the Grahams and Tom and Mary —

CASS Do I know any of these folk?

HARRY Course you do. Remember old Jack Kirk out at the end of the town?

CASS Yeah, sure.

HARRY Well, this is his son and his wife. And d'you remember Goldpark Lodge?

CASS Colonel Johnson's place? He's not alive, is — ?

HARRY No, no; the Grahams bought it.

CASS The whole estate? Boy, they must be swank, huh?

ALICE They own a dance-hall here. (*To* HARRY) Is that swank?

HARRY And the Dohertys and the Tobins and the Wallaces —

CASS (*Too casually*) I don't know none of them. But I'll pitch in. Any of the Crowleys knocking about still?

ALICE I don't think so.

HARRY Crowleys? No, moved to Dublin — oh, years ago. Con married a girl from there. Did very well for himself, too. And we'll have the Doyles and Bill Morgan and — (CASS *is moving around the room again, staring in admiration*)

CASS Boy, Harry, you made out good, huh?

HARRY Not bad, Cass.

CASS And you tell me you don't work at the accountancy no more?

HARRY Not for fifteen, twenty years. I didn't have the time.

CASS Gee, I'm so glad for you. I was always worried in case — you know — with momma living with you and all the kids getting education — like I thought you mebbe didn't have much to fling around. But this! Boy! (ALICE *whispers to* HARRY)

HARRY I wasn't much of a letter writer, Cass.

CASS You were just great, Harry. (*To* ALICE) You know he actually wrote me when Father died. Wasn't that something?

HARRY I know, I know, I know, and I apologize.

CASS If it hadn't ov been for you (ALICE) the whole family might ov been — in the Jays.

HARRY And I should have written to thank you for all the money you sent; every month without fail.

CASS Forget it.

HARRY No, I won't forget it. And I want to talk to you about it now.

ALICE We never really thanked you properly.

CASS I had no use for it.

HARRY Only this morning I was checking up: ten dollars every month for fifty-two years —

ALICE Not to talk of the children's birthdays and Christmas presents and —

CASS I couldn't help making it. Honest. It just kept dropping into my lap.

HARRY There would have been no point in telling you we really didn't need it: you would have sent it all the same.

CASS Not now, Harry. (*Looking round again*) It's — it's elegant, that's what it is.

HARRY Thank God we were never in want. In the beginning Mother's salary was adequate, and then I qualified and went into practice, and I had a few lucky ventures.

CASS I would only have scattered it anyways.

HARRY What troubles me now, though, is that perhaps you were the one who needed it, and not us.

CASS It got candy for the kids, didn't it?

ALICE Don't keep her in suspense. Tell her what you did.

CASS I sent a few bucks 'cos I wanted to. So forget it. Okay?

HARRY I checked this morning. And over all the years — including birthdays, anniversaries, Christmas and all — you sent 7,419 dollars — something over two and a half thousand pounds. And that's not counting interest.

Enter DOM *and* MOTHER. *They stay upstage.*

CASS Boy, that would ov bought me one hellova head! Momma, how are you, Momma? Kid.

HARRY Don't think we don't appreciate the sacrifices you made. We do, all of us —

CASS (*To* MOTHER) Tell him to shut up, will you? He's boring the hell outa me.

HARRY No, this must be said. When you went out there first ten dollars must have been a lot of money.

CASS (*Getting really tired*) Harry —

HARRY However, to get back to what I was saying: we saved it for you, Cass.

CASS ?

HARRY It was all banked, every penny of it from the very beginning. As I said, we never really needed it. And now it's all intact, for you to use as you wish.

ALICE It's a nice little nest-egg.

HARRY And it makes you independent of everyone.

ALICE We've been planning this as a surprise.

HARRY How you're fixed financially is your own affair, but this will provide a nice supplement to whatever you have. I'll give you the pass book tomorrow morning.

ALICE And I'm warning you to keep an eye on this scrounger. (DOM) Don't let him wheedle a halfpenny from you!

CASS (*Almost whispering*) None of it . . . never bought nothing?

HARRY If we had needed it. But, thank God, we never did. The important thing is not the money itself, Cass — it's not all that much — but the knowledge that you are not dependent on anyone. That's what it gives you.

CASS Dependent?

HARRY You can crack your fingers at all of us!

CASS The kids' birthdays . . . and the doc's bills . . . and Father Tom's education . . .?

HARRY I assure you, Cass, we never wanted for anything. And we're as grateful as if we had used it.

CASS walks away from them. She is slowly trying to take in what she has been told. Pause.

ALICE Cass . . .?

CASS I could ov bought myself a mink coat! So! I could ov put a fan in the bedroom in the summer! Yeah! Another thing — I could ov eaten prime beef every Sunday!

ALICE We thought you'd be delighted.

CASS wheels round on them, madly, desperately elated. She speaks almost at full voice.

CASS There was only one story would make Jeff laugh — you know? Brave as a lion but, Jeeze, that leg of his gave him hell at times; and when he would get away down there he would say to me, 'Tell me the story about the Irish Mick, Cass'. And I would stroke his forehead and tell him, see, and he would laugh and laugh even though he heard that story hundreds — millions of times —

MOTHER This is indeed a festive occasion.

CASS Boy, is she psychic! You know the story, Alice? About the Irish kid comes over to the States, see, and after three months he writes back to the folks: 'I've been made floor manager of this store. This is a feather in my cap'. And the folks back home they're thrilled, see, even though there's no dough in the envelope. And three months later he writes again: 'I've been made manager of the whole plant. This is a feather in my cap'. Again no dough, but the folks is pleased for him, see. And three months later another letter: 'I've been made president of the company. This is a feather in my cap'. (HARRY *laughs — an attempt at normality.* CASS *almost spits her anger at him*) You haven't heard the punch line yet! What the hell are you laughing at?

HARRY I just thought — president after nine months —

41

CASS And then they don't hear from the kid for months and months, see, not a line; until finally they get this air letter, very urgent, and written inside is: 'I'm broke. Please send fare home'. And the kid's pop he gets pen and paper, and he clears the kitchen table, and he writes back, 'Stick the three feathers up your ass and fly home!' (*Only* DOM *laughs.* ALICE *turns to him rapidly*)

ALICE Take Mother to her room at once!

Exit DOM *and* MOTHER.

HARRY Cass, this sort of —

CASS When you planning to have this party? I'll supply the champagne — I got money, haven't I? And I'll sing and dance and I'll tell stories and I'll have all the Kirks and Colonel Johnson and all the Crowleys and all of them rolling in the aisles. (*To* ALICE *who is about to leave with the tray of drinks*) Come back with that hooch, honey! I'm only warming up!

ALICE *leaves.*

HARRY Cass —

CASS I got more stories than Bennett Cerf ever heard of — about cannibals and girls with Chinese tattoos on their bellies and about elephants and marooned sailors — hell, that's all Slinger ever done was tell me stories. He was a bum, okay, but he had lovely teeth. Like the one about this guy that comes home drunk every night and his wife she's about sick of him. You know that one, Harry?

HARRY Cass, this sort of talk —

CASS So sick that she can't stick it no more. Anyways, this night the guy comes home plastered again and falls across the bed and starts snoring. And the wife she has this empty candy box with a great big blue satin rosette on the lid, and she takes the rosette off the box and goes over to the bed and takes the guy's trousers off and ties the bow to his rice crispies. And the next morning when he wakes up first thing he sees is this big blue rosette.

And the wife she says to him, 'Where were you last night?' And the guy he scratches his head and he says, 'Jeeze, honey, I don't know. But wherever I was I got first prize'.

HARRY I'll speak to you later, Cass.

He marches off. CASS, *left alone, suddenly slumps into a chair. The false elation is all gone, the anger all dead. She is on the verge of tears.*

CASS I never wanted no gawddam mink coat! And I hate prime beef! And fans they give me the sinus! As for air conditioning — Gawd — you can keep it, keep it. . . . I don't want it . . . not a cent of it! . . . (*Fumbles for cigarettes, her hands shaking*) Some guy, Slinger, I'll tell you, some hellova guy. . . . (*Lights cigarette. Shades her eyes against the lights and searches the auditorium*) You still out there? Stick around and we'll have fun together. You'll see, lots of fun. . . .(*Looking around set*) Where the hell *is* everybody? (*To audience*) You wanta know why I never got married? 'Cos I hadn't time — that's the why — working — and then I sorta fell in with Jeff, and we had our own arrangement. He was no sweet guy but he liked me — I know he did — he never said it but I know he did. And when he died, well what d'you do but come home. . . . That's what it's all about, isn't it — coming home? Why the hell does he call it *The Loves of Cass McGuire?* A gook title, I'll tell you!

She hears TRILBE *approach and takes out her compact and makes up. While she does this she keeps her back to* TRILBE.

CASS Hi.
TRILBE Catherine, m'dear, what are you doing?
CASS (*Brisk, busy*) Getting ready for the ball.
TRILBE Are we having a ball?
CASS Why not. Where's Fred Astaire?
TRILBE I beg your pardon?
CASS Mr. Ingram — he not about?

TRILBE He's in the chapel.

CASS Got religion all of a sudden?

TRILBE Catherine, I think you should know: today is the anniversary of his wife's death.

This shocks CASS *into normality. Pause.*

CASS Gee, I didn't know she was *dead.*

TRILBE Very tragic. Very, very tragic.

CASS When did it happen to her?

Enter INGRAM, CASS *stares at him.*

TRILBE Some other time. . . . (*Briskly*) Tell us about the catering business in America, Catherine.

CASS (*Watching* INGRAM) Sure, sure, it was something . . . you bet . . . I worked in this . . . this downtown restaurant . . . you know, all big shots; and I was . . . sort of like a head waiter only I was a woman, you know. . . . Hi, Mr. Ingram.

TRILBE That must have been fascinating employment.

CASS You bet . . . yeah . . . Mr. Ingram. . . .

INGRAM Good afternoon.

CASS Mr. Ingram, it has just come to my knowledge that you are bereaved of your spouse. . . .

INGRAM Yes. Yes.

CASS And I would like you to understand that I am deeply grieved on your behalf.

INGRAM It was a long time ago.

CASS Was it T.B. or the cancer, Mr. Ingram? Jeeze, the number of women I know that went down with the cancer — boy, you could ov packed Radio City with them.

TRILBE I think it is milder today, don't you?

INGRAM Stella was drowned, Miss McGuire.

CASS Gawd.

INGRAM Forty-six years ago. I will tell you about it.

He moves towards the winged chair and sits.

TRILBE Mr. Ingram —
INGRAM On our honeymoon.
TRILBE Mr. Ingram, dear, should you . . . today . . .?
INGRAM I will tell you about it.
TRILBE Very well then.

Gently fade in Wagner's Magic Fire *music. Then, after a few seconds,* INGRAM *continues.*

INGRAM I was twenty and she was eighteen, with hair golden as ripe wheat —
TRILBE A ballet dancer.
INGRAM And after the wedding we went to Salcombe —
TRILBE In Devon, in the south of England.
INGRAM And every night in the hotel I played the piano and she danced and danced and danced —
TRILBE Her hair swinging behind her.
INGRAM And I played and played, faster and faster —
TRILBE For her dancing, dancing.
INGRAM — until her eyes shone with happiness and the room swam with delight and my heart sang with joy —
TRILBE Oh, the dancing, dancing.
INGRAM And during the day we walked across the moors —
TRILBE Hand in hand.
INGRAM — and kissed and loved and ran and danced —
TRILBE Across the windy moors.
INGRAM — because my prize was a young prize, with hair golden as ripe wheat; and there was music in my ears, throbbing, heady, godly music. . . .
TRILBE Away, away to the end of the promontory.
INGRAM Where we kissed and danced and loved. . . .
TRILBE Poised above the waves.
INGRAM And then —
TRILBE And then —
INGRAM And then, one day, running before me, calling to me, she slipped. . . .
TRILBE His Stella —
INGRAM And there was no sound.
TRILBE His star.
INGRAM No sound but the sound of the sea. And for nine days

45

they searched —
TRILBE Probing with long poles.
INGRAM — from a German yacht that was fishing there; he was a prince.
TRILBE His dancing Stella.
INGRAM Swirling in the water, loose, being nosed by fish, her hair loose, her limbs loose. . . .
TRILBE His dancing star.
INGRAM But they never found her. And the German yacht sailed away —
TRILBE On a spring morning.
INGRAM — away to the Mediterranean, to the sun . . . with hair golden as ripe wheat.
TRILBE Leaving them together, in Salcombe, in the south of England.
INGRAM My prize, my bride. . . .
TRILBE His dancing bride.
INGRAM My dancing, swirling bride.
TRILBE Our truth.
INGRAM 'But I, being poor, have only my dreams — '
TRILBE 'I have spread my dreams under your feet — '
INGRAM 'Tread softly because you tread on my dreams.'
TRILBE Our truth.

They hold their positions for a few seconds; then INGRAM *rises.*

INGRAM It is such a mild afternoon . . . I . . . I think we'll walk past the refectory and along . . . it's a very pleasant little. . . .

He goes towards the door.

TRILBE A splendid idea. Wait for me, Mr. Ingram. (*She goes with him, but hesitates before she exits and turns to* CASS) Join with us, Catherine. Join with *us*.

They go off. Fade out music. CASS *stares after them. Her reaction this time is not too violent. She is more perplexed, more puzzled. She talks to herself.*

46

CASS Jee-sus! What d'you know about that! (*Fumbling for a cigarette*) As if those Germans couldn't find a needle in a haystack, for Gawd's sake! (*To audience: far from confident*) Hi! . . . Stick . . . stick around. . . . This'll be okay, you'll see; this'll all sort itself out . . . I dunno . . . this gawddam going back into the past! Who the hell knows what happened in the past! Joe Bolowski he thought he was a gawddam pianist! . . . Jeeze, how do I know . . . maybe he was. . . .

ALICE *appears in the shadows upstage.* CASS *does not look at her and her answers are automatic.*

ALICE My father was always a gentleman, Cass, wasn't he?
CASS Sure . . . sure. . . .
ALICE There were rumours, malicious rumours, about him; but they weren't true, Cass, were they?
CASS A gentleman, honey. That was Joe Connor.
ALICE But there were whispers, and they were carried to me after his death.
CASS One of the most respected men in town.
ALICE He was, wasn't he?
CASS Sure.
ALICE And dignified, and scholarly, and courteous?
CASS You can say that again.
ALICE (*Grandly*) Yes, of course he was. One of the old families.
CASS Old as the Hudson.
ALICE Yes, the old gentility. They may not have had wealth but they had background. And background's so important.

She disappears into the wings.

CASS (*Turns, appealing*) Alice, honey. . . . Momma? . . . Harry? . . . Father? . . . Connie, Connie?

She is about to wander into her bedroom when PAT QUINN *makes his usual brisk entrance.*

PAT Wonderful! Wonderful! Wonderful!
CASS Pat! Gee, am I glad to see you, Pat! Where have you

47

been?

PAT I told you all along but you never believed me!

CASS We'll have a party, Pat; and I've got presents to hand
out; and I'll get Buster Ingram to play the piano and —

PAT He's coming for me this day week — him and the wife.

CASS Sure, Pat; you're only temporary —

PAT You won't believe me. You never did. But he's just after
leaving the door. He took my trunk away with him. Look
— the receipt from the matron! 'Paid with thanks'. A
split new house with a room and all for me. In a week, on
his way home from the monthly meeting.

CASS (*Totally deflated*) On the level?

PAT I knew you never believed me. You thought I was only
blathering like yourself. But there it is in black and
white. Ask Tessa. She helped me out with the trunk.

CASS (*With quiet venom*) You dirty bastard!

PAT Ha-ha-ha-ha-ha, we see the true colours now! The big
swank American lady, Mr. McGuire's sister! Aha but
you never fooled me, McGuire! A skivvy — that's what
you were — written all over you! And a drunken aul'
skivvy, living in sin with a dirty aul' Yank that kicked you
out in the end!

CASS Shut up!

PAT But what else would you expect. Didn't your aul' fella do
the same in Scotland. And we all know your stuck-up
aul' mother that never paid a bill in her life. Oho, I know
youse all right — tramps turned respectable! Respectable, how are you!

CASS Shut up!

PAT Who'll carry in your drink now? Aul' raving Costello?
Aul' mad Ingram? Cripes, you'll be a prize trio. The
people'll be paying to come and look at youse!

CASS Shut up, you bastard! Shut up!

PAT Oh, the lady-like Miss McGuire! Oh, the sweet lady!
Good luck to you! It won't be long till you start raving,
too! Rave away, woman! You'll be in good company!

He skips off. CASS, *angry, sobbing, rushes into her
room, takes the bottle from under the mattress and
drinks. Throughout all this business she is mumbling*

48

incoherently to herself. Then she lights a cigarette and then makes up.

CASS Jeeze, the fun Jeff and me had that day we went to Coney Island . . . Lincoln's Birthday, 19 and 27 . . . that's when it was . . . we laughed and laughed and laughed, that day on Coney Island. . . . Connie . . . Connie. . . .

The room is too lonely. She rushes back to the common-room. Through the French windows we can see TRILBE: *she beckons to* CASS. CASS, *too, sees her, and swings round to the audience.*

TRILBE Catherine!

CASS shades her eyes and searches the auditorium.

TRILBE Catherine!
CASS (*To* TRILBE) Leave me alone, will you? (*To audience*) They think they're going to run me back into the past but by Gawd they're not. . . . I live in the present, Harry boy, right here and now. Where are you? Stick with me.
TRILBE Catherine!
CASS Go away! Go away! Gooks . . . real gooks living in the past, but not Cass McGuire. (*To audience*) If things get too rough I can go and hide in the signal box. I've always got places I can go to . . . always . . . you bet . . . a dozen of them . . . out to the crooked bridge . . . at the back of the mill. . . . But the signal box . . . it's the safest . . . no one ever looks there. . . . Where are you? Jeeze, where are you?
TRILBE Catherine!

She now stands strained between the calling voice and the audience. Her mouth forms words but no sound comes. We wait for her to break down. Then, in a voice that is firm and clear, she calls.

CASS One black coffee and one salad sandwich? You bet. Coming right up, sir. Coming right up.

Quick curtain. End of Act Two.

49

Act Three

The evening of Christmas Eve. CASS *is lying asleep on her bed. She is partially dressed.* TRILBE *and* INGRAM *are sitting at the table. He is writing a letter and she is reading the paper. Silence.*

TRILBE You are concentrating too deeply on that letter. You'll end up with a headache.

INGRAM If I could only have a little quiet. . . .

TRILBE I used to suffer from migraine once. (*She reads*) Imagine that!

INGRAM Mm?

TRILBE The temperature in Sydney yesterday was 97 degrees.

INGRAM Really.

TRILBE I had a brother in Sydney. Peter.

INGRAM Yes?

TRILBE A diver.

INGRAM What did he dive for? (*This has never occurred to* TRILBE *before*)

TRILBE I beg your pardon?

INGRAM What did he dive for?

TRILBE How would I know what he dived for, Mr. Ingram? He was a diver — a diver — a diver. And a professional diver — just dives, doesn't he?

INGRAM I . . . I . . . I suppose so. . . .

She goes on reading. He goes on writing. CASS, *without opening her eyes, stretches out a hand, feels under the mattress, finds a bottle, puts it to her mouth. The bottle is empty. The hand throws it away. She drops off again.*

TRILBE A report of Brother O'Rourke's funeral. Two bishops and three ministers of state.

INGRAM Who's that?

TRILBE I told you about him yesterday. Principal of Fairhill
Secondary School. A Kerryman. A very . . . athletic
principal.

INGRAM I remember.

TRILBE 'He is survived by three sisters and three broth—' Surely
that's a misprint!

INGRAM Hm?

TRILBE I presume it should read three sisters and three brothers.
He would never have left three brothels, would he?

Enter TESSA *with a notebook and pencil. She is looking
very much more alive and quite smart.*

TESSA Matron says would youse rather a concert or a fillim
tomorrow night?

INGRAM I . . . I really don't. . . .

TRILBE A concert or a film; let us analyse this. Who would be the
artists in the concert?

TESSA How would I know. The fillim is called —

TRILBE Film, child. One syllable. Film.

TESSA — *General Custer's Last Stand.*

TRILBE That sounds familiar. (*To* INGRAM) Who was General
Custer?

INGRAM Wasn't he one of the leaders of your Easter Rebellion?

TRILBE I do believe you're right. (*To* TESSA) Yes, I vote for the
film.

INGRAM So do I.

TESSA (*Holding out her left hand*) And none of youse noticed.

TRILBE What?

TESSA Look.

TRILBE Chilblains, m'dear?

TESSA I'm engaged. He gave it to me last night.

TRILBE Well I'm delighted. I wish you every happiness.

INGRAM *rises from the table, goes over to* TESSA, *takes
her hand, and kisses her fingers. Throughout this brief
ceremony* TESSA *is at first embarrassed, then giggles,
and then is oddly moved. As he does this:*

INGRAM May I? (*Kiss*) A long and contented life to both of you.

TESSA He's a building contractor by trade.

TRILBE A very practical profession, too.

TESSA Well, he's not a real contractor, yet.

TRILBE But he's a fully fledged tradesman?

TESSA He will be when he finishes his apprenticeship, and until he sets up on his own he's working as a bricklayer for Harvey and Todd. But he's going to go out on his own in the spring . . . after we're married.

INGRAM That will be very . . . he'll do well, I'm. . . .

TESSA And the first thing he's going to do is build a bungalow for us, with bay windows and venetian blinds, and a big garage and a red-tiled roof. I think a red roof's nice.

TRILBE Indeed.

TESSA We have a site and all in our head but we're not telling anybody where it is in case the price would be stuck up. And as soon as we're settled in comfortable I want youse two and Miss McGuire to come out and have high afternoon tea with us.

TRILBE That will be something to look forward to.

TESSA We're going to do all the entertaining before the babies start coming. I'll put Miss McGuire down for the fillim, too. (*At door*) The aul' woman to fill Pat Quinn's place has just arrived. Her name's Lizzie Butcher. She's crying her eyes out. Wouldn't you think at her age she wouldn't mind where she'd be?

> *She goes swinging off. There is a flatness after her departure, the first of a series that drain the atmosphere of all life and buoyancy.* INGRAM *and* TRILBE *return without interest to their tasks.*

TRILBE Bungalows are all very well if you are positioned on a rise. Otherwise there is no privacy.

INGRAM They'll have venetian blinds, she said.

TRILBE You're quite right. (*Pause*) She must be resting. I haven't seen her all day. Have you?

INGRAM Have I what?

TRILBE You can be so stupid at times! Have you seen Catherine?

INGRAM No . . . no . . . I haven't.

TRILBE (*Hesitantly*) Did you get the impression last night, Mr. Ingram, did it occur to you that Catherine was slashed?

INGRAM Good heavens! Slashed?

TRILBE Inebriated. Did that occur to you?

INGRAM Miss McGuire? Certainly not. I would be very shocked. (*Pause*) What made you think so?

TRILBE Nothing. Nothing at all. Probably I imagined it.

INGRAM I'm certain you did.

TRILBE Very well. I did. Let's not discuss it any further.

> *They continue reading and writing. Then suddenly* TRILBE *has a revelation.*

Pearls!

INGRAM ?

TRILBE That's what people dive for! That's what Peter dived for! Peter dived for pearls. Round the rugged rocks the ragged rascals ran. My brother Peter dived for precious pearls. Little Tessa should practise on that type of exercise.

> HARRY, ALICE *and* DOM *enter. Dressed for an outing. They carry presents.*

HARRY We're looking for Miss McGuire. Matron said she would be here. (TRILBE *and* INGRAM *pay no attention*) Excuse me. . . .

TRILBE Good evening. Very cold, isn't it?

ALICE Where could we find Miss McGuire?

TRILBE We haven't seen Miss McGuire all day, have we, Mr. Ingram?

INGRAM That's . . . that's what we were just saying.

HARRY Would she be in her bedroom? I'm her brother.

INGRAM Her bedroom is just down the passage.

HARRY (*To* ALICE) I'll see if she's awake first.

> HARRY *goes down front.* DOM *follows him at a distance.*

ALICE We brought a few chocolates for all the inma— for all the residents.

TRILBE Do you know Brother O'Rourke, m'dear?

ALICE I've heard my sons talk of him.

INGRAM Thank you for the —

TRILBE Well, he's dead, and we're puzzled by the report of his funeral. He had three sisters; that we know; but what we wish to establish is this: had he any brothers?

> ALICE, INGRAM *and* TRILBE *go into mute conversation.* HARRY *stands beside Cass's bed. He speaks to her in a quiet, tender voice.* DOM *stands at a distance, tense, alert.*

HARRY Cass. Cass. It's me, Cass. Harry.

> CASS *stirs slowly. Then sits up. Automatically gropes for cigarettes. Lights one with shaking hands. She looks and feels a wreck. Stares vaguely at her immediate surroundings on stage. Talks listlessly to herself.*

CASS Where the hell is everyone?

HARRY Cass. . . .

CASS Gone . . . gone. . . .

HARRY It's Harry, Cass. Alice is outside. We brought a few things for you. Slippers. Fruit.

CASS Boy, what a dream. Like it kinda went on and on every time I closed my eyes. . . .

HARRY You're very comfortable here. And it's so cold outside. Snow's forecast.

CASS We're on this big ship, sailing home to Ireland, see . . . all laughing and singing and dancing and drinking . . . all the gang of us that used to get up the concerts for the White Cross and the boys on the run and the church building and the prisoners' fund back home . . . and we're having that much fun, all sailing for home. . . .

HARRY Cass. . . .

CASS And they're all milling about; and there in the middle of them — Jeeze and was I glad to see them! — there's Joe Bolowski and Slinger having a ball to theirselves; and Joe, he sees me standing up there in this big long white wedding dress, and he shouts up to me, 'Cass,' he shouts, 'I'd pull no chain on that'. And everyone laughs and laughs and laughs, even Father O'Neill. Boy, he should ov been in the marines.

HARRY We're going to have a quiet Christmas after all, Cass. The children, it seems . . . it seems they can't come. Betty sent a telegram and Tom phoned this morning. Naturally they're very disappointed. So I suggested to Alice —

CASS Gawd, am I hung over!

HARRY I was wondering would you like to come out to us for tomorrow . . . and Boxing Day . . . and perhaps for a day or two more. . . .

CASS Jeff he never has a head 'cos he drinks four pints of iced water before he goes to bed. Sez it makes the alcohol float to the top. Hell, I dunno; but a head's better than running to the ur-eye-nal all night.

HARRY I'd give everything I have, Cass, anything, just to be able to put a coat around you and drive you home with me. But when a man gets married . . . and we've had Mother for so long . . . although Alice couldn't have been kinder to her. . . .

CASS *swings her feet out of the bed. The effort sets her head throbbing.*

CASS Oooooh . . . oh-oh-oh . . . Gawd. . .!

HARRY I don't suppose you know about them, Cass, but she has her worries . . . we both have . . . we haven't heard from Aidan for seven years, not since he went to Switzerland; she worries a lot about that. And then Betty's marriage isn't just as happy as . . . as . . . Even Tom at times . . . the seculars didn't suit him and we gather that he's restless again even though. . . . You really are better off here, Cass.

CASS During Prohibition there was this hooch called Tiger's Piss. One swig of that stuff and you thought you were Anna May Wong. Oooooooooooh. . .!

HARRY I'll call again tomorrow. And every week. I promise. (*He takes a half-bottle of whiskey from his pocket and leaves it at the foot of the bed*)

CASS I dunno what I drunk last night. But I guess that tiger's still operating.

HARRY Good-bye, Cass. A happy Christmas.

He goes reluctantly back to the common-room. After he has gone CASS *finds the bottle he left.*

CASS Well, I didn't know I had that much foresight.

As she is drinking, DOM *darts forward and sticks his face up to Cass's right ear. His eyes are burning with disgust.*

DOM You're nothing but a dirty, rotten, aul' — aul' — aul' — !

He cannot finish. He runs into the common-room and then off.

HARRY Dom? (*Sternly*) Dom!

ALICE What happened to him?

HARRY He's probably — Where are you going?

ALICE I'll only be a minute.

HARRY There's no point in disturbing her.

ALICE I'll meet you at the car.

HARRY For heaven's sake, Alice, she's not —

ALICE I said I'll only be a minute. See where Dom has gone to. (HARRY *does not want a scene before* TRILBE *and* INGRAM. *He smiles blankly at them, apologetically, and mumbles*)

HARRY The compliments of the season to you. I'll be in again tomorrow or the next. . . .

TRILBE And a very merry Christmas to you, sir.

HARRY looks uneasily after ALICE and then goes off to find DOM. ALICE has moved into Cass's bedroom and stands beside her. CASS is totally unaware that she is there.

ALICE (*Warmly, leaning over*) It's me, Cass. . . . I know Harry has told you: none of the children. . . . (*She checks herself in time: straightens up: continues with a control that is touching in its rigidity. She is on the point of tears*) The children are all coming — all of them — Betty and Tom and Aidan — arriving tonight — late — a real family gathering. You'll like Aidan; he's — you know — unorthodox — his artistic temperament — always moving from job to job — always getting into little scrapes. Oh, you'll love him. And Tom. People say he's like my father; remember? But then Father was a more sort of scholarly man, wasn't he? He'll make an excellent bishop; great administrative ability. And Betty and the baby. We haven't seen it either, you know; our only grandchild. They turned out well, didn't they, Cass? And Harry worked so hard for them. (CASS *makes a quick movement and her head explodes*)

CASS   Jeezus!

ALICE   They're a consolation to us, Cass, aren't they?

CASS   (*Sings*) 'Oft in the stilly night 'ere slumber's chains have bound me
Fond memory brings the light of other days around me.'
(ALICE *makes a tentative gesture towards* CASS *again*)

ALICE   Cass. . . .

CASS   Best mayor New York ever had.

> ALICE *withdraws. She dabs at her nose, straightens herself, and dashes out of the bedroom and through the common-room.*

TRILBE   And a very happy Christmas to you, too.

ALICE   (*Vaguely*) Oh, yes . . . yes. . . .

> She goes off.

TRILBE   That was Catherine's brother and his wife and their youngest child. They also have a son an architect in U.N.O. and a daughter a doctor, married to a London specialist, and a son a Jesuit.

INGRAM   I'm not deaf, you know.

TRILBE   A very satisfactory family. (*She opens the paper again. Then stops*) It's coming back to me now: he led a flying

column in Tipperary!
INGRAM The Jesuit?
TRILBE General Custer.

CASS *puts on her shoes. She takes a drink and feels better. Completes her dressing. She gets to her feet and is about to go into the common-room when she hesitates, takes a few steps towards the footlights, shades her eyes, searches the auditorium. She sees nobody.*

CASS And I could ov swore there were folks out there. (*Shrugs*) What the hell.

She shuffles into the common-room. TRILBE'S *vigour makes her feel even more sour.*

TRILBE Ah! There you are!
CASS Hi.
TRILBE We've missed you all day. (*Quietly*) He's very upset with the income-tax people. They have confused him with some other Meurice Ingram, a professional wrestler.
INGRAM Good evening. (CASS *waves casually to him*)
TRILBE And now, Catherine, I want your advice. Where would be the best place to display my Christmas cards? (*Delving into bag*) I didn't want to keep them selfishly in my room. I was thinking of the walls —
CASS Sure.
TRILBE — or the mantelpiece. Or what about stringing them across the window? I've got some green tape here, too.
CASS Yeah, that's fine, fine.
TRILBE You Americans have such novel ideas about decoration. Here we are! Some of them are so pretty this year. (CASS *takes them listlessly*)
CASS Five?
TRILBE There are certainly more than that. (*Searches bag again*) Two more. And I'll get another from Mother Benignus of Loreto. She never has time to do hers until after the Christmas rush. What do you think?
CASS Well, as the broad said to the senator, you can't —

58

(*Recovering quickly*) — I think mebbe we'll just be old-fashioned and set them up along here (*the mantelpiece*). Okay?

TRILBE Yes. Yes, perhaps you're right.

CASS goes downstage and searches for the audience again. Finds no one.

CASS No one. Must have been dreaming.

TRILBE What's that, m'dear?

CASS The folks — I guess you were right.

TRILBE Never mind, Catherine, you have us. Our world is real, too.

INGRAM Our world is just as real.

PAT comes on singing. He is carrying two cases. He is at the top of his form.

PAT 'Adieu, adieu, kind friends adieu, adieu, adieu, I can no longer stay with you, stay with you . . .'

The other three go absolutely flat. They watch his antics with dead eyes, almost as if he weren't there.

(*Rapidly*) It has been a pleasure knowing you all. And only that the nephew can't manage without me — he's outside in the car there with the missus, waiting for me — you'd never drag Pat Quinn away from Eden House and the good company and the grand food. Miss Costello, a very happy Christmas to you and the very best of good luck. Mister Ingram, sir, it has been an honour knowing you and being educated by your fine talk. Good luck to you. Miss Mac, we had our differences, Miss Mac, but that's all over and done with. (*Softer*) And if you want me to make an arrangement with Sweeney — you know where — I'm your man, d'you understand?

TESSA (*At door*) He says if you want to stay that suits him.

PAT Coming, darling, coming. The season of goodwill and forgiveness and all; and if ever you want anything done for you outside in the great big world just drop a note to

Mister Patrick Joseph Quinn, Esquire, care of Mister John Quinn, Esquire, Cloughmore, and I'll see you right. A happy Christmas, one and all, and a bright and prosperous New Year, and may all your dreams come true. (*At door*) By the way, you're getting a slice of ham each for tea.

> *He exits. The silence now is total, the depression complete.* INGRAM *takes off his glasses and polishes them.* CASS, *her back to the audience, fingers the cards.* TRILBE *gets a handkerchief and blows her nose vigorously. Pause. Then high unnatural talk bursts.*

TRILBE I think perhaps my favourite piece for children is a little poem I once came across in a magazine during my travels. It is called *Clickety-clack,* and I have recommended it to dozens of pupils:
'Clickety-clack, clickety-clack, goes the puffing train on the railway track;
Bearing us off on a mystery tour,
And when we'll arrive we're never quite sure. . . .'

INGRAM When he was a young barrister my father published a pamphlet attacking capital punishment, and that was . . . oh, fifty years ago . . . or more. . . .

TRILBE 'We puff over meadows and rivers and streams
Till we come, puffing gaily, to the land of our dreams;
And there we are happy to wander and roam
For we feel so content in this land that is Home. . . .'

INGRAM Long, long before the movement ever became popular. He was a stern man but I think he was a just man . . . in his own way. . . .

TRILBE We're having ham for tea.

INGRAM Snow is forecast.

TRILBE And turkey tomorrow.

INGRAM I don't suppose it'll lie.

TRILBE And a film at night.

> *They cannot sustain talk any longer. Silence flows in and fills the room. Then, suddenly,* CASS *with great effort and courage springs into activity.*

CASS   Hello! It's Christmas Eve, isn't it? I almost forgot! What are we all moping for? (*Begins searching in one of her bags*) I got some things in here. Sometimes I think I carry the whole of Macy's around with me! Yeah, yeah, here we are. (*Formally*) Mr. Ingram, a very merry Christmas to you. (*Gives him a parcel*)

INGRAM   Is it — ?

CASS   Sure, sure, go ahead. It ain't a Cadillac nor nothing like that. But you might like it.

INGRAM   I haven't had a Christmas present, Miss McGuire, since . . . oh, for . . . for. . . .

CASS   Agh, it's nothing; only a pair of — (*She suddenly realizes that she has given him the wrong present. She snatches it back from him again*) Jeeze, gimme that back! It's okay, okay, keep calm, keep calm, Father Christmas is still coming; I still got something for you, only I was giving you the wrong thing, see! (*Produces another packet*) And that wouldn't ov been real smart, huh? This is more like it. Yeah, this is it, okay.

INGRAM   I'm deeply moved, Miss McGuire.

CASS   How the hell can you be moved till you see what you got? It ain't no Cadillac neither, I can tell you. 'Cos they didn't have the colour I liked. (*To* TRILBE) I got something for you, too; an accessory for to match along with your pink sweater. Pretty nice.

INGRAM   (*Displaying socks*) Thank you very, very much. They're . . . they're. . . .

CASS   Yeah, they're a couple of socks. Health to wear. You know like I kinda figured you do a lot of walking past the refectory and along the . . . you know. Only don't bring them back to me to mend. I'm not the sewing type.

The new resident, MRS. BUTCHER, *enters left and walks across stage to the exit right. She is small and old and perky. She is carrying a tiny cardboard case in one hand and a handkerchief in the other. She walks with hesitant courage because she is confused, unsure, timorous, and yet defiant. Because of her uncertainty her manner appears to be challenging. Immediately at her heels is* TESSA *carrying her bed clothes.*

TRILBE Good evening to you.

She looks at TRILBE *and quickly at the others but does not answer and does not slacken her pace. When she goes off* TESSA *puts her head back again.*

TESSA Mrs. Butcher, a bed-wetter if ever I seen one!

CASS (*Impetuously*) Hi. Kid.

TRILBE I would hazard a guess that our friend is not of a jovial disposition.

CASS You kinda liked these, I think. Catch. Go on. Take it. It ain't rat poison.

TESSA It's not the flowers, is it?

CASS Take them away before I get mean again. And a happy Christmas to you.

TESSA And the same to you, Miss McGuire. And thanks very much. No matter what the matron says, I knew you were a lady. (*Exits*)

CASS Well, you can tell the matron from me that if she was on fire I wouldn't — Agh! Now what did I do that for!

TRILBE She's engaged, you know.

CASS Matron?

TRILBE Tessa. She's going to be married in the spring.

CASS Yeah? . . . In the spring? . . .

INGRAM They're an excellent match for my new suit.

TRILBE The Christmas atmosphere is really building up. (CASS *has nothing for* TRILBE *now except the gloves*)

CASS (*Busily*) Yeah, and I got something for you, too, Trilbe, like I said . . . you bet . . . and I gave it some thought . . . and finally I came to the conclusion that what you needed most —

TRILBE An accessory.

CASS A pair of warm gloves — that's what it is — 'cos this place, hell, it would freeze the hair off a bald man. So that's what I went and got you — a pair of woollen gloves — mebbe a bit on the big side, but they'll shrink, won't they? Warm — woollen — gloves — and a happy Christmas to you.

TRILBE Like Mr. Ingram, Catherine, I'm speechless, I really am.

CASS That's a change.

TRILBE I'm deeply grateful to you. Thank you.

CASS Forget it. (*An awkwardness descends. The brief elation dies*) And that's about it. Everything's gone. All my worldly goods. (*Looking into bag*) Nothing left.

CASS *returns to the mantelpiece. The silence flows in. To stop it:*

INGRAM Mr. Quinn was a . . . a . . . he was a light-hearted man.

TRILBE He has gone, Mr. Ingram.

INGRAM I know. I know.

TRILBE To a nephew who owns a substantial farm.

INGRAM He told me.

TRILBE He never really belonged, you know.

INGRAM In a way.

TRILBE Oh, no; he was never fully one of us.

INGRAM I suppose not.

TRILBE A willing little man, I'll grant you, but never one of us. Don't you agree, Catherine?

CASS *moves away from the mantelpiece. She is looking at one of the cards. For the first time she is vague, dreamy, remote. And when she speaks all brashness is gone from her voice.*

CASS One Christmas I saw a man in a green sledge in Central Park, and he was being pulled along by two beautiful chestnuts. He must ov been a very rich man to keep two chestnuts in Manhattan, I'll tell you. And the horses they had these bells on their harness, you know, like music . . . . (*She goes forward to the winged chair and stands beside it*) And as he was passing me he happened to look over. And do you know what he done? He lifted his black hat to me. . . .

TRILBE (*Softly*) Tell us, Catherine.

CASS There's nothing to tell, really . . . just a man with a kind face and two chestnuts and a green sledge and the white of the snow and the music of the bells . . . and he looked at me and he lifted his black hat to me, that gentleman in Central Park did. . . .

TRILBE Tell us.
INGRAM Tell us.
TRILBE Tell us.

> CASS *suddenly bursts into tears and drops into the winged chair. There she cries and groans, covering her face with her hands while the spasm lasts. Then, emerging from it, she sits up straight, almost with nobility, and very slowly lets her head come to rest on the back of the chair.*

TRILBE Perhaps you should read to us, Mr. Ingram.
INGRAM I never get a chance to finish.
TRILBE Tell us the end of one of your stories, then.
INGRAM I'll finish the Tristan story. I know it by heart.

> *Fade in slowly and with growing volume 'The Liebestod' from* Tristan and Isolde. *After a few seconds of the music* CASS *begins to speak. She becomes more and more assured, as if the recounting of the events made their memory and their accuracy more vivid.*

CASS I stood at the stern of the ship, and two white and green lines spread out and out and out before me. And the gentleman I worked for, Mr. Olsen, he was only a few years older than me, tall and straight and manly, with golden hair and kind soft patient eyes. And I had two dimples. . . . (*Very rapidly: suddenly agitated*) What — what — where — what am I — ?
TRILBE No, no, go on, go on. Golden hair and patient eyes. And you had two dimples. . . .
CASS (*Relaxing*) Yeah — yeah — two dimples. . . . And he would ma. ɛ me laugh and put his fingers into the dimples and say, 'Hooked you, Baby'. And the morning we got married my father he stood up and sung *Oft In The Stilly Nights 'Ere Slumber's Chains Have Bound Me,* and people there said if he had ov been a younger man he would ov made the big time, he was that good, my father; and Mr. Joseph Bolowski, he played classical tunes on the piano; and Mr. Slinger, he was the toast-

master; and everyone was so gay, so gay. . . .

INGRAM 'But even though they were separated by exile Tristan's love for Isolde grew; and finally he sent for her.'

CASS And we moved into this great ten-roomed apartment on the West side, and from our bedroom window we could see the ships sailing off to South America and the Bahamas . . . and Ireland . . . and Glasgow . . . And all round the walls were pictures of Harry's kids; I was their Auntie Cass, you see; and regular as the clock came their letters — I have them all — fine kids. . . .

TRILBE A doctor, a priest, an architect, a student.

CASS And when I came back home they were all down at Cork to meet me; and Harry and Alice and Momma; and Connie, he wanted us to stay over with his folks in Dublin but Harry wouldn't hear of that; and all the cars drove up, one behind the other, like it was a parade or something, some of them with chauffeurs and all, right up Harry's big wide avenue, underneath all them golden chestnuts, and all our friends came in and we had such a party. . . .

INGRAM 'And at his bidding she came to him on a ship. But he, wounded on his couch, was too weak to meet her. And she got off the ship and rushed to his side and embraced him. And he died in her arms.'

CASS And Connie and me we slipped out by the back and went for a walk out to the crooked bridge and he said to me, 'Do you remember, Cass? Do you remember?', as if I ever forgot, even for a second. And we must ov spent so long out there that Harry, he got worried and went searching for us, and the police they were searching, too. And when we got back the party was over, and the house was quiet, and Momma, she and I had a long chat together, private, confidential, my Momma and me. And then I told Harry that I was going to move out 'cos I wanted to be independent; but he wouldn't listen to me, not Harry, he's too stubborn. But I insisted. So we bought this place close to the sea and we fixed it up and Harry's kids, they come to see us all the time and play around on the beach; and we work and work and don't have no time to think. . . .

65

INGRAM 'And she died, too, of love. And from their grave two rose trees grew up and intertwined so that they could never be separated again.'

CASS Connie and Father and Harry and Jeff and the four kids and Joe and Slinger . . . and I love them all so much, and they love me so much; we're so lucky, so lucky in our love. (*To* TRILBE) What is it you say?

TRILBE 'But I, being poor — '

CASS '— have only dreams. I have spread my dreams under your feet.'

INGRAM 'Tread softly — '

CASS '— because you tread on my dreams.'

TRILBE Our truth.

INGRAM Our truth.

CASS Our truth.

The music fades. Enter MRS. BUTCHER.

BUTCHER (*Too loudly*) Good evening to you.

She goes immediately down front and sits on an upright chair, her back resolutely to the others. She opens a magazine and pretends she is reading. She addresses the audience confidentially.

BUTCHER My God, would you just look at them! If you met them on a dark night you would think you were doting.

The gong goes.

TRILBE Ah! Teatime! And how are you, m'dear? (BUTCHER *realizes she is being addressed*)

BUTCHER What — what's that?

TRILBE You're well, I trust.

BUTCHER Nothing wrong with me. Thanks be to God I was never a burden to anybody.

INGRAM *and* TRILBE *get their things together to go off for tea.*

TRILBE (*To* BUTCHER) We're having cold ham for tea this evening. Sometimes rather tasty. And General Custer tomorrow night.

BUTCHER (*Directly to audience*) Our Lady of the Seven Snows!

TRILBE A film of the Ninety-eight rebellion.

BUTCHER (*To audience*) Lunatics is sane compared with these ones!

INGRAM (*To* TRILBE) Would the lady . . . is she . . .d'you think she would care to . . . to . . . to . . . to join us?

TRILBE (*To* BUTCHER) The dining-room's along here, m'dear.

BUTCHER Carry on. I can look after myself.

INGRAM (*To* TRILBE) Perhaps I should . . . should I . . .?

TRILBE Much too soon. She's still at *that* stage. Catherine?

CASS Yeah — yeah — coming — sure.

TRILBE (*To* INGRAM) I do believe I'm getting the Christmas spirit fully now. (*Sings*) 'Good King Wenceslas looked out . . . .'

> INGRAM *joins her and they exit singing.* CASS *sees* BUTCHER *sitting alone and crosses to her.*

CASS You gotta eat, you know. You can't go without your vittles.

BUTCHER I can look after myself, thank you very much. (*To audience*) Has she a drink on her?

CASS My name's Olsen, by the way. My late husband — mebbe you heard of him — General Cornelius Olsen — he made quite a name for himself in the last war. But you just call me Catherine.

BUTCHER (*To audience*) Full!

CASS I dunno, but I think it's better to get into the routine here right away. (*Coaxing*) You'll like the tea they make. It looks like horse's — it looks like it was treacle, but it sure has a kick.

BUTCHER You just run along now and have your meal.

> CASS *hesitates. She is conscious that she has some intelligence she could communicate, if only she knew what that intelligence were.*

CASS When I first came here —

TESSA *appears at the door.*

TESSA (*To* BUTCHER) You! You're wanted in the matron's office
to sign some forms.
BUTCHER If you're addressing me, my name happens to be Mrs.
Elizabeth Butcher, and I'm accustomed to —
TESSA And she says be quick about it.
BUTCHER (*Directly to audience*) Maybe I should keep on the right
side of that matron one. Not that I'll be here for long.
(*Rises to leave*) Stay where you are. I'll be back in a
minute.

She goes off right with pathetic dignity.

TESSA You! You're going the wrong way. Matron's office is
back.

BUTCHER *leaves.*

CASS She'll learn, sweetie. She'll learn.
TESSA Huh! And the airs of her! You'd think she was
somebody! (*Suddenly coy: drawing* CASS'S *attention to
the artificial flowers she was given as a preliminary to
showing off her ring*) Nice?
CASS Elegant.
TESSA And what about that? (*Ring*)
CASS What?
TESSA Engaged.
CASS Well, well, well!
TESSA (*By rote*) It's a solitaire diamond surrounded by a cluster
of dazzling rubies and mounted on plat-ig-num and gold.
(CASS *catches her hand and searches earnestly*)
CASS Where's the diamond?
TESSA God, are you blind, too? There!
CASS Oh yeah — yeah — so it is. Gee, that's nice, sweetie.
(TESSA *moves away, lost in contemplation of her ring*)
Would you do me a favour?
TESSA (*Not listening*) What?

68

CASS I got this only brother, see, Harry, and I expect he'll drop in to see me some time this evening, you know, for Christmas and all; and I want you to tell me as soon as he comes, sweetie, 'cos I don't want that matron to turn him away or nuthin'. That would hurt him. And make a big fuss about him, honey, will you? All his days he's been kicked around. Treat him like he was important, you know.

TESSA He old, too?

CASS Harry? No, Harry's not old. But he's one of those guys — you know — he never got nuthin' much outa life. Just the two of us, and I guess he didn't have it good. I was the one that made it.

TESSA We're going to spend our honeymoon in Glasgow.

CASS You'll keep an eye out for him, sweetie?

TESSA All right. (*Leaving*) Come on. Your tea's ready.

CASS (*To herself*) Poor, poor Harry. . . . (*She sighs at* HARRY'S *bad luck. Then brightens, looks around the common-room with calm satisfaction*) Home at last. Gee, but it's a good thing to be home.

She lifts her bags that she always carries, takes another contented look around, and goes off singing her own version of Good King Wenceslas.

Curtain.